The Journal of Agent Gin...

Phase Three Resistance, Rebellion & Redemption

Published by Write Impression Ltd.
Copyright 2024 Linda Deane, Gina's Flower Queen Portrait by Furryroyal
ALL RIGHTS RESERVED
No part of this publication may be reproduced, stored in a retrieval system transmitted in any form or by any means, electronic, mechanical, photocopying, recording or otherwise, without prior written permission from the publisher.
ISBN 978-1-7385812-5-2

DO NOT READ PAST THIS POINT UNLESS YOU'RE A CAT!!!

Dear Reader,

If you haven't read my earlier diaries, you may find yourself confused about some of the things I'll be mentioning in this one. Here's a brief recap of some key points.

My name is Gina Ginger Knickers and I'm an agent of Planet Cat. Planet Cat is the mysterious place from which all cats come and to which they eventually return. Certain select hoomins get to go there too. I believe it goes by the name of Heaven to some hoomins, but we cats simply call it Planet Cat.

I was made by G.O.D. (the Generator of Design) who put me in this cute, furry earth suit and assigned me the very important mission of bringing joy and laughter to the daily lives of all hoomins on Planet Earth (and to keep an eye on them, of course), especially Linda and Mr. D, our minions at Castle Deane where I and my feline companions reside.

I'm tasked with filing regular reports to Planet Cat, and in these private journals – which are STRICTLY for feline eyes only – I record my daily contemplations, observations, and activities to jog my memory when compiling the reports. Unfortunately, I don't have much space in this notebook, so I can only provide a highly summarised overview. You'll need to refer to my previous journals to understand some of the context or to look anything up. Here's where you could obtain your copies:

The Library of Feline Congress, Planet Cat

or **https://amazon.com/author/lindadeane**

or you could email us at **cats@deanes.co.nz** and let my purrsonal assistant, Linda, attend to your query.

Purrs and head boops!

Gina GK

1 August 2021

A new week, a new month, and a new journal!

I love Sundays and I love new things. I'm looking forward to filling the pages of this new notebook with all sorts of interesting information. Who knows what this month will bring? One thing I know for sure is that I've got my work cut out helping Callie tell George's story.

Before we begin on that great saga of romance, I'd like to put it on record that I'm innocent. Apparently, someone sharpened their claws on the side of the couch. Linda has no way of knowing how long these marks have been here. They could have been made by anyone! Ages ago! I really don't know why she's asking me about this. I hope she doesn't think I did it. I would never!

She can't just go making accusations and implying things like this! Sheesh, lady!

> Claw marks? On this couch, you say? Are you sure, Linda? Nope. Sorry. I have no idea how they got here. Have you asked Callie?

FELINE ROYALTY

PRINCESS GINA

2 August 2021

Last night I overheard Linda and Mr. D talking about me. He asked her what she was planning to feed "the Little Princess" for dinner. They could only have been talking about me. I had no idea! I'll have to look into my ancestry ASAP! Perhaps I should insist that Callie calls me Princess Gina, or Your Royal Highness, or Your Majesty. I may very well be entitled to it. She's not the only queen in this house, after all. And I should insist on a purple velvet pillow.

3 August 2021

Callie is so mean! I raised the subject of my royal pedigree, and she nearly rolled her bulk off the couch laughing. She says they always refer to us as princesses or queens. It's just a thing they do. But I don't believe her! I AM a real princess. I am. I am. I AM!!!

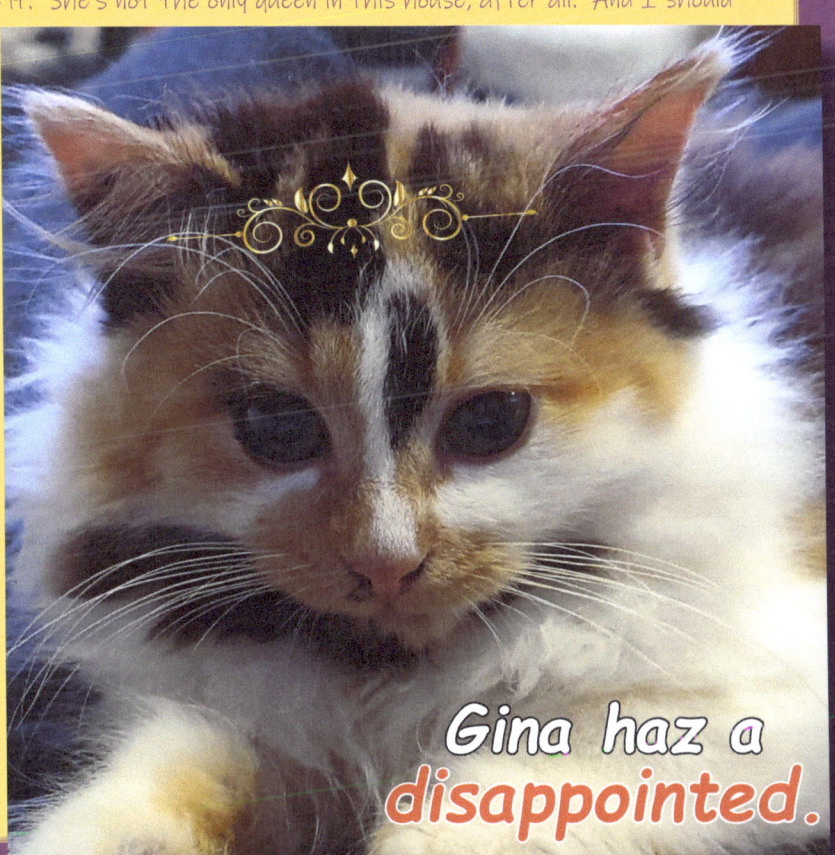

Gina haz a disappointed.

Of course I heard you calling me, Linda. Can't you see me ignoring you?

4 August 2021

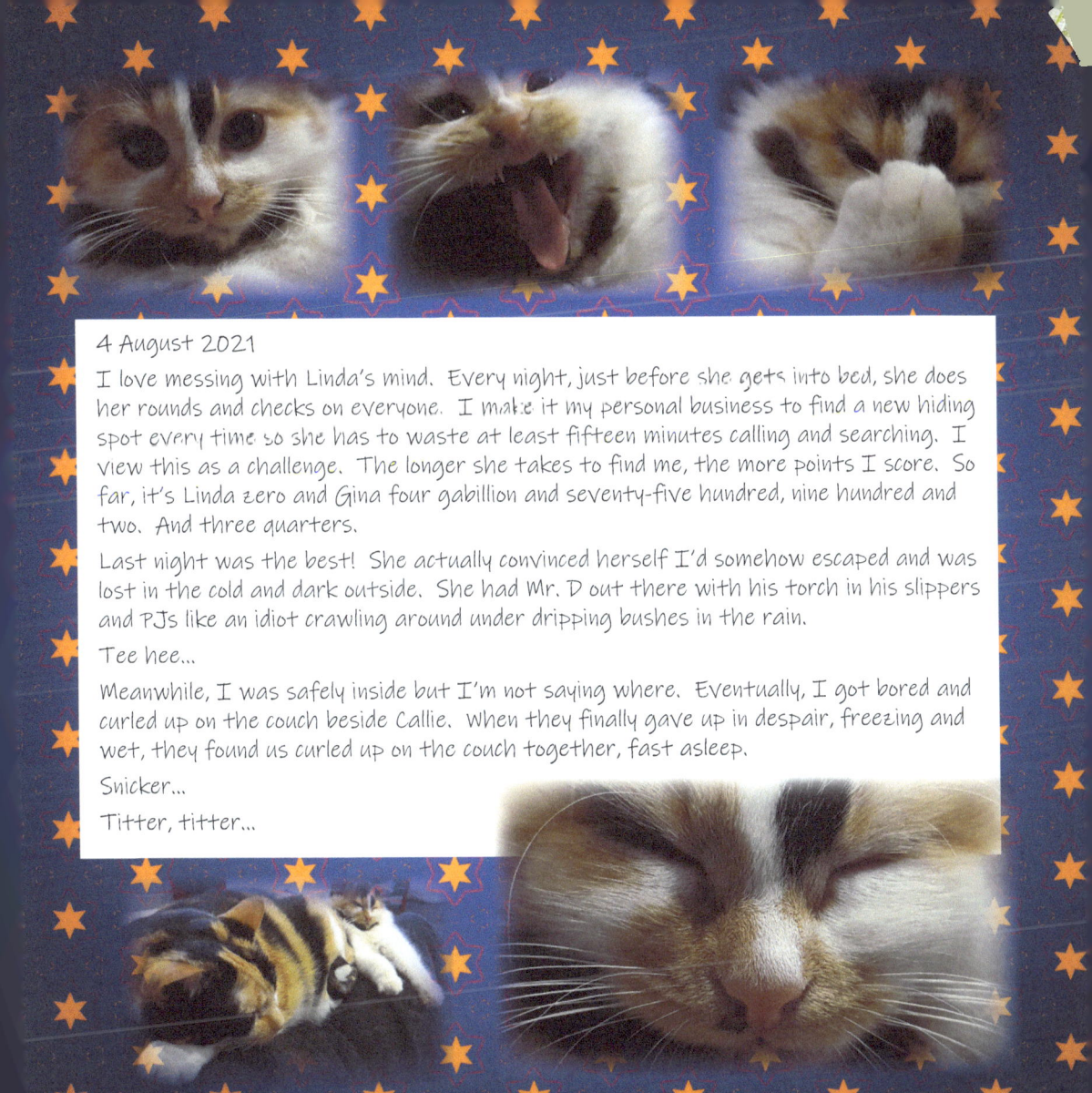

I love messing with Linda's mind. Every night, just before she gets into bed, she does her rounds and checks on everyone. I make it my personal business to find a new hiding spot every time so she has to waste at least fifteen minutes calling and searching. I view this as a challenge. The longer she takes to find me, the more points I score. So far, it's Linda zero and Gina four gabillion and seventy-five hundred, nine hundred and two. And three quarters.

Last night was the best! She actually convinced herself I'd somehow escaped and was lost in the cold and dark outside. She had Mr. D out there with his torch in his slippers and PJs like an idiot crawling around under dripping bushes in the rain.

Tee hee...

Meanwhile, I was safely inside but I'm not saying where. Eventually, I got bored and curled up on the couch beside Callie. When they finally gave up in despair, freezing and wet, they found us curled up on the couch together, fast asleep.

Snicker...

Titter, titter...

5 August 2021

The issue of the dancing platform came to a head today and I won. Finally!

This is – and always will be – primarily my dancing platform/sunbed/garden viewing deck etc. In fact, it can be anything I choose. Henceforth, it will only function as a surface for hoomins to eat their noms as and when absolutely necessary, but I still don't see why they can't eat on the floor as we do.

Furthermore, Linda may only sit here with her laptop under my supervision and guidance when I'm instructing her.

I may be small, but I am mighty. Raaaawwwrr! Hear Gina roar!

6 August 2021

When will they learn that resistance is futile? Hoomins in rebellion can be very tiresome.

I am Gina. Yes, my mission is to bring them joy, but I am in charge here and they will have to accept this. Sooner rather than later.

I WON'T go to bed when Linda tells me to. Good luck to her if she persists in trying to catch me and put me in my bed. If I wanna run zoomies all night, I can and will!

Your point of view? Nope, I still can't see it. Sorry, Linda.

PS: If I wanna toss my noms in the air and drag it all over the kitchen floor, I will. Just 'cos I can!

I LIKE making food art.

7 August 2021

Today I learned: Tea

Linda went out and I had to keep myself entertained. When she got home, our conversation went something like this:

> Linda: "So, what did you do today, Gina?"
>
> Gina: "I learned the catnip mouseys ta swim. In my small water bowl. And in Callie's big water bowl too."

I didn't tell her about my new friends. She doesn't believe in Moppy's fairies, so I doubt she'd believe me if I told her about the fantastic creatures I met after I drank the catnip tea.
Callie promised she wouldn't tell either.

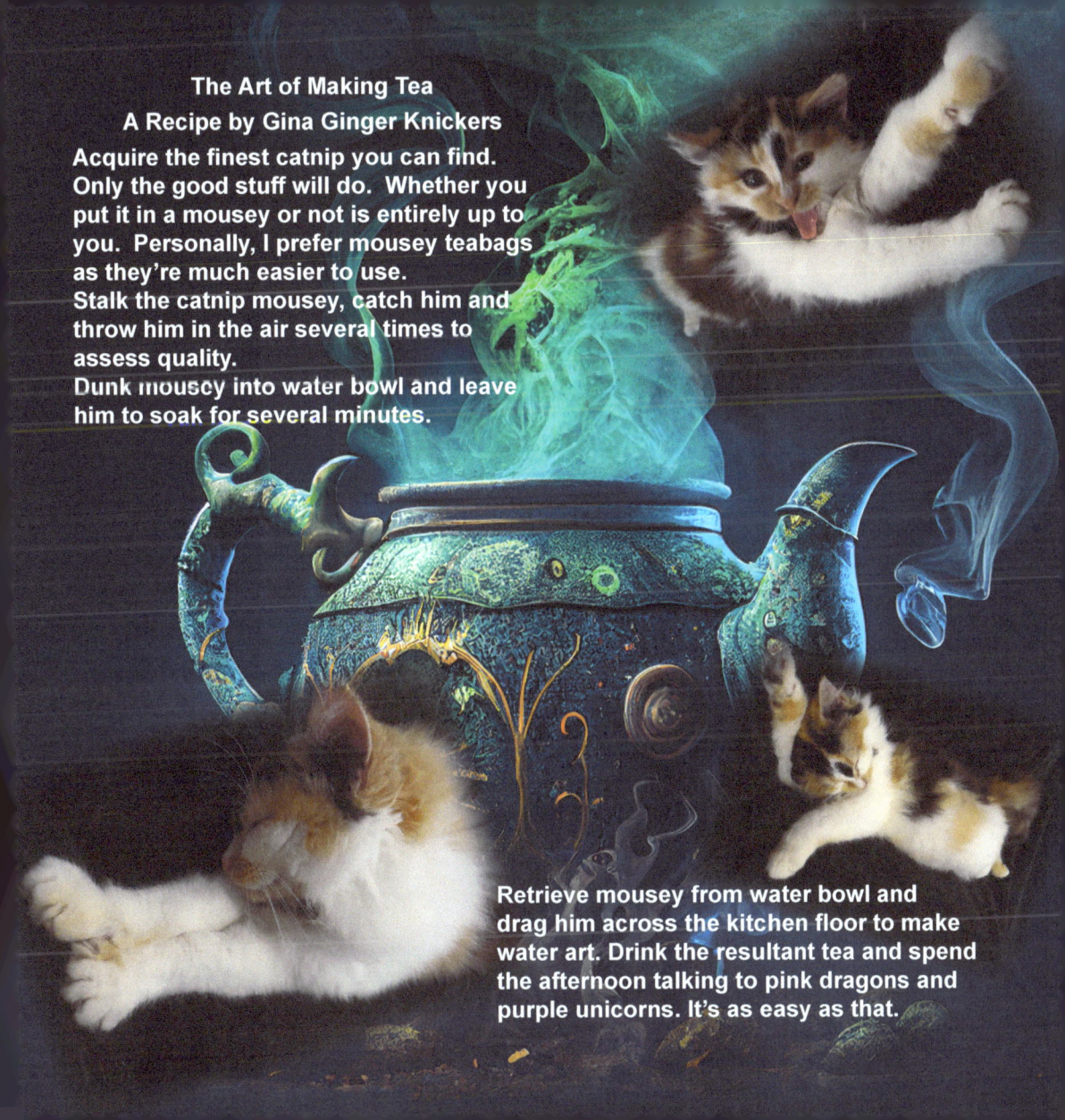

The Art of Making Tea
A Recipe by Gina Ginger Knickers

Acquire the finest catnip you can find. Only the good stuff will do. Whether you put it in a mousey or not is entirely up to you. Personally, I prefer mousey teabags as they're much easier to use.

Stalk the catnip mousey, catch him and throw him in the air several times to assess quality.

Dunk mousey into water bowl and leave him to soak for several minutes.

Retrieve mousey from water bowl and drag him across the kitchen floor to make water art. Drink the resultant tea and spend the afternoon talking to pink dragons and purple unicorns. It's as easy as that.

8 August 2021

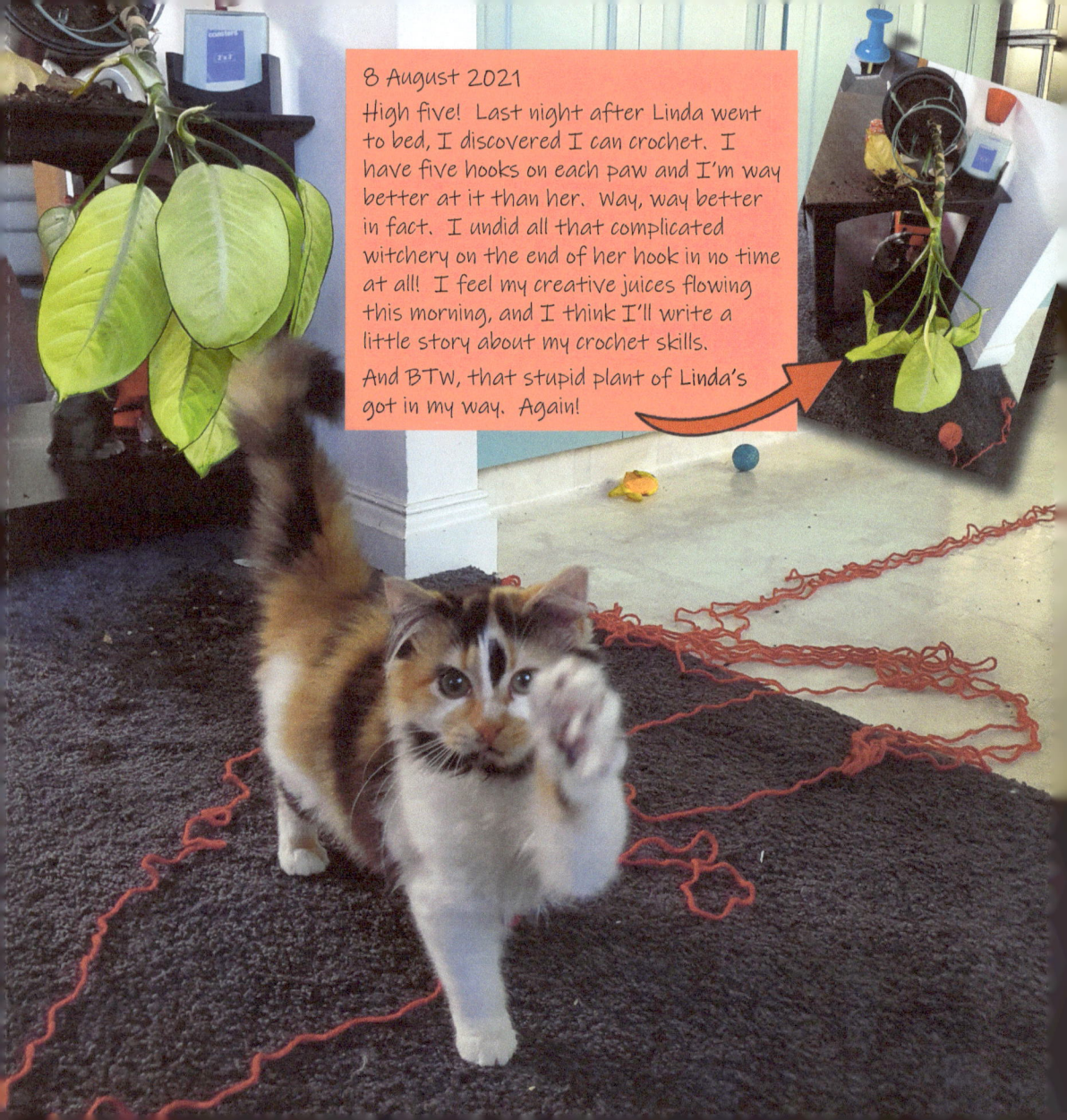

High five! Last night after Linda went to bed, I discovered I can crochet. I have five hooks on each paw and I'm way better at it than her. Way, way better in fact. I undid all that complicated witchery on the end of her hook in no time at all! I feel my creative juices flowing this morning, and I think I'll write a little story about my crochet skills.

And BTW, that stupid plant of Linda's got in my way. Again!

The Crocheting Cat - A short story by Gina Ginger Knickers

Once upon a time in a cozy castle, there lived a beautiful princess named Gina. Gina was no ordinary feline; she had mastered the magical art of crochet.

Every night, mesmerised, she carefully observed the crazy old witch performing magic, twisting the yarn around the enchanted hook. In, out, up, down went that hook. Right before her eyes, Gina witnessed the ball of yarn shrinking as the witch conjured up a blanket.

One night after the witch had taken her magic potion (a cup of chamomile tea) and fallen into a deep sleep, Gina secretly read the precious blanket spell lying on the table next to the witch's chair.

Row 1: 2 hdc in 3rd ch from hook, 2 hdc in the next ch, hdc2tog 4 times, *2 hdc in each of the next 4 chs, hdc2tog 4 times; repeat from * across until the last 2 ch. 2 hdc in each of the last 2 ch. Turn. (144 sts)

And so on and so on and so on...

But Princess Gina had her own built-in crochet hooks and her own method. She did not need the complicated spell. With her skilful little paws, she managed to undo the witch's sinister work in a matter of minutes. And just for good measure, she trailed the unravelled yarn from the lounge to the dining room, to the kitchen and beyond, creating her own fantastic designs as she went.

Word of Gina's magical crochet prowess spread throughout the land, and everyone marvelled at her whimsical creations. Her boundless imagination had astounded them. She had charmed them with her "supernatural" crochet skills. And so, in the heart of Castle Deane, the legend of Gina the Enchanting Crocheting Cat was born – a tale spun with laughter, colourful yarn, and the charm of a cat who believed in the magic of her imagination, one intricate stitch at a time.   THE END

10 August 2021

Generally, Callie and I get on very well, but sometimes she can be very selfish, especially in the evenings when Linda and Mr. D put their feet up for some rest and relaxation in front of the magic window[1]. She always claims the best spot on Linda's lap.

We had a bit of a disagreement last night. I asked politely if she'd consider heaving her bulk off to one side. I won't repeat what she said but these pictures speak volumes!

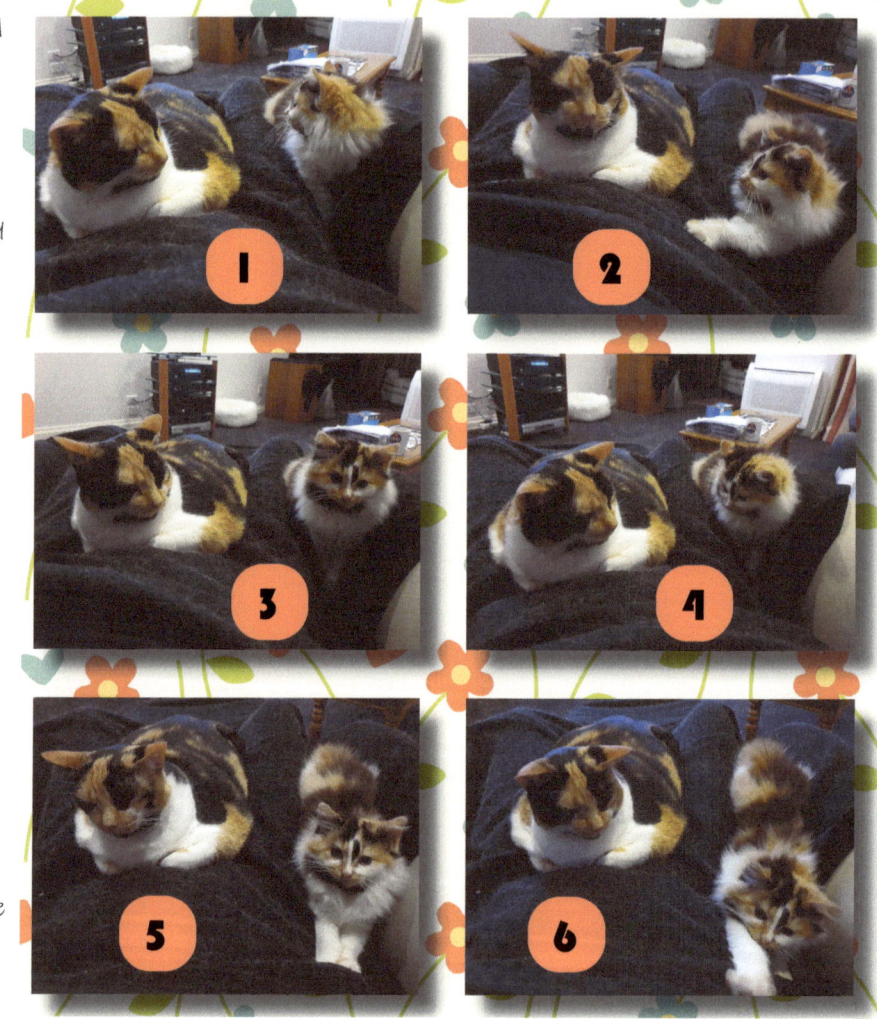

[1] See The Journal of Agent Gina Ginger Knickers (Phase One: Advent and Subjugation), p.20, A Guide to Gina-Speak, Part 2

11 August 2021
Guess who got to the lap first this evening? Callie had to sit with Mr. D. She was so mad!

This is bullship, Linda! DO something! #$%&@

Surely you're not planning to eat the WHOLE bag of chippies by yourself, Linda?

12 August 2021
I live with very selfish hoomins. Linda, in particular. She never shares her snacks with me. I've registered an official complaint with the C.O.M.P.E.T.E.[2] about this. The hearing ought to be soon, and then will come a day of reckoning.

[2] *See The Journal of Agent Gina Ginger Knickers (Phase One: Advent and Subjugation), p.5, A Guide to Gina-Speak, Part 1*

13 August 2021

I know I've spoken about it before, but the service around here is appalling! What do I have to do to get my meals served on time?

I'm thoroughly sick and tired of glaring at my empty nom bowl or staring pointedly at that clock on the wall. Linda is as thick as a pile of floofy blankets straight out of the dryer. She simply cannot pick up subtle hints. I have to scream my head off to get her attention and even then it still doesn't register with her that I want my noms and I want them NIAAAAAOOOw, now, Linda, NIAAAAAOOw!

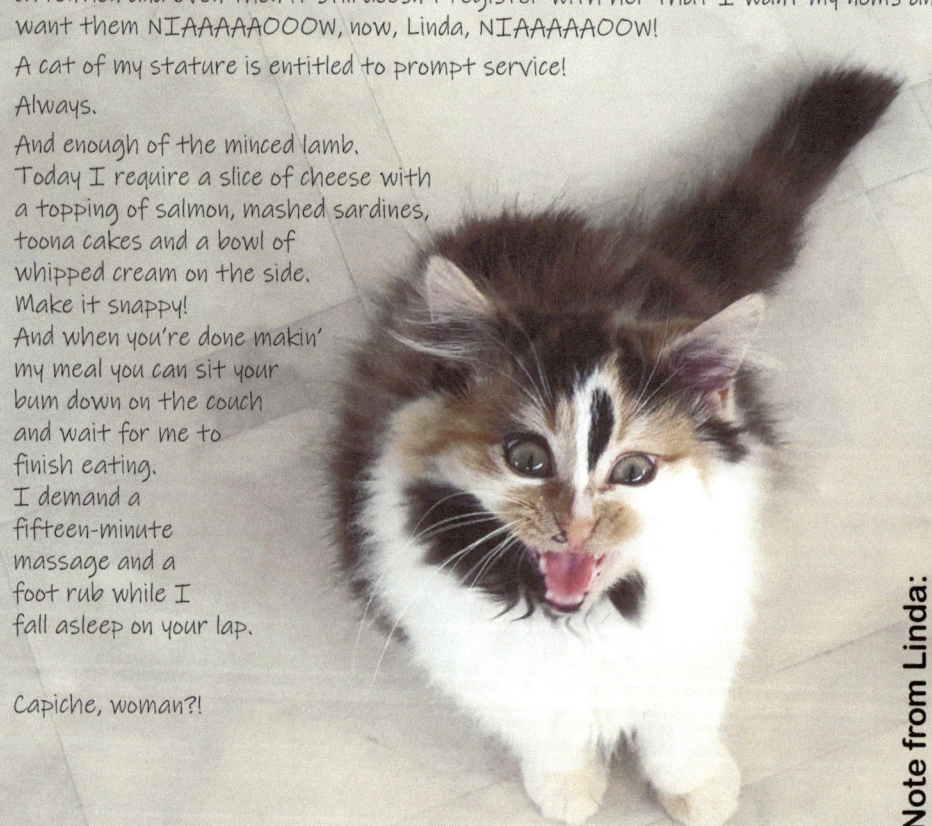

A cat of my stature is entitled to prompt service!

Always.

And enough of the minced lamb. Today I require a slice of cheese with a topping of salmon, mashed sardines, toona cakes and a bowl of whipped cream on the side. Make it snappy! And when you're done makin' my meal you can sit your bum down on the couch and wait for me to finish eating. I demand a fifteen-minute massage and a foot rub while I fall asleep on your lap.

Capiche, woman?!

Note from Linda: Time out in the naughty corner coming right up for little Miss Ginger Knickers!

14 August 2021

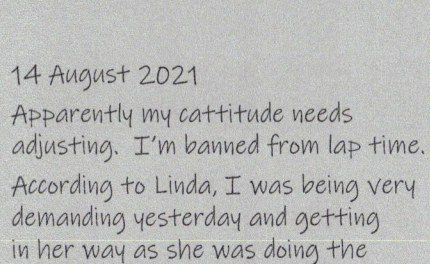

Apparently my cattitude needs adjusting. I'm banned from lap time.

According to Linda, I was being very demanding yesterday and getting in her way as she was doing the housework. So, she put me in the crate.

I'm shattered.
Just...
Devastated!

Surely I'm more important than dusting and cleaning and dishes and laundry? She can do all those stupid things after my bedtime if she must.

Must attempt an escape tomorrow. That'll learn her!

15 August 2021

I had a long chat with my sister, Judi. She knows exactly how to handle Linda and Mr. D. She gave me some good tips (see page opposite). Judi is the naughtiest cat in our household, and quite possibly the naughtiest cat in New Zealand. Maybe, even the world! I'm very proud to call her my sister. Judi is an expert in training kittens and other cats how to naughty. Foster kittens come from far and wide to learn from the master.

But she's also very, very good at managing hoomins, particularly Mr. D. She has him wrapped around her pinky claw. Linda, not so much. That woman is quite a difficult case. Even Judi thinks so.

Four Basic Principles of Hoomin Training by Judi Jonsdottir Deane

#1: Pretend you are deaf. This is really very easy. Simply ignore anything and everything they say.

#2: Keep training sessions short. Hoomins cannot maintain focus for more than two or three minutes, 5 at the most. Even if you're thoroughly enjoying the ear skritch, after a minute or two, discipline your hoomin with a sharp nip.

#3: Use small treats to reward good behaviour. A well-timed hairball is always received with great joy. As is a poo or two just outside the litter box.

#4: Timing is everything. Schedule training before important events. Hoomins are far less likely to resist your training if they're about to begin an important Zoom call with colleagues.

16 August 2021

Judi's advice does not seem to be working as well as I'd hoped. I tried ignoring Linda, but she ignored me back. And when I nipped her fingers, she flicked me on the nose. Ouch!

She scolded me for kicking the litter out of the litter box when I rewarded her for serving my noms on time for a change, and she put me in the bathroom and shut the door on me when I tried to get her attention by climbing up her leg while she was on the phone.

So much for Judi's advice. Hmph…

17 August 2021

I decided I'm going to do my own thing. Gina goes where Gina likes! And Gina does what Gina pleases!

Nawty Gina breaks all da rulz !

18 August 2021

Well, that didn't go as planned. I really thought I'd make a statement by stomping on the dining room chairs with my foot needles. Clearly, it wasn't the statement Linda wanted to hear from me 'cos I'm back in the crate tonight.

Perhaps it's time to rethink my strategy.

little angel

Gina iz a *good* kitteh.

19 August 2021

I decided today I'm turning over a new leaf. I'm going to be Nice Gina from today onwards. No more Naughty Gina. It won't be easy 'cos I like doing my own thing, and I don't like submitting to authority. But rebellion is evil. And I have it so good here in this house. Things could have been very different for me. I could still be living out in the wild with no shelter, searching for food. It's better to be appreciative and mindful of the good things we have. From now on I will have an attitude of gratitude. No more cattitude.

I will make Planet Cat proud. I will make George proud. I'm so grateful he arranged this assignment at Castle Deane for me.

Goals for today:

Wait patiently for noms.

Cover poo neatly. Don't kick the litter out of the box.

Keep foot needles in. Especially on the couches.

Let Linda's visitors pet me.

Don't wash their stink off my fur immediately after they have touched me.

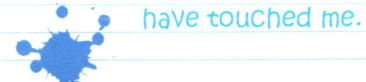

Reminder: Be respectful to Callie.

Reminder: Be obedient to Linda (and Mr. D).

20 August 2021

I love Callie's butt. It's as big as a bus, so it's not practical for us to lie side by side on Linda's lap, especially since I'm growing so fast. We've come to a good arrangement now.

She moves right up to the top of the lap which leaves room for me between Linda's calves when she's in the recliner with her feet up.

The reason I like Callie's butt so much is because it's made of warms. On these chilly August nights, a big warm butt against your back is a bonus. Callie's big butt is one of the benefits of living here at Castle Deane and I'm grateful for it.

21 August 2021

Mr. D is very fond of his speakers, and he likes to listen to music on the weekends. I've expressly been told NOT to sharpen my claws on the speakers. Old Gina, the naughty one, used to do it when nobody was looking, just for fun. But New Gina, the good one, has made a big effort to resist this very enticing temptation. I almost did it, but then I remembered in time and stopped myself on the very brink of that particular precipice. I think I deserve an ice cream. I hope they bring one home for me when they get back from their walk on the beach.

22 August 2021

Linda was working on George's book with Callie, but I had to interrupt her. I told her she better come see what happened in the kitchen.

The cupboard was open and the treat box had fallen off the shelf and ka-sploded all over the kitchen floor. I tried very hard, but I couldn't clean it up all by myself.

Burrrp... 'scuse me.

23 August 2021

Something terrible happened today. Terrible, TERRIBLE! I nearly STARVED! I had nothing to eat for two hours! I was WEAK with hunger.

You see, I wanted to know what mysterious things they keep in the garage, so I snuck in behind Linda when she took a load of washing into the laundry at the back of the garage and she didn't see me dart under the big scary wheelie box.

I've seen Linda and Mr. D inside that wheelie box. I think it's called a "car," but I'll have to check with Callie. I've watched from the kitchen windowsill as it carries them down the driveway and off to mysterious and exotic places. They always come back, though. Sometimes they're only gone for a short while, other times they're gone for ages and ages.

So, while I was hiding under the wheelie box, Linda went out of the garage and shut the door. I was trapped! It was very interesting at first. I found two dead flies on the windowsill, some smelly old boots in the corner, covered in yucky dried mud, a nice box to sit in, and a rag that smelled just awful – like the big scary wheelie box. Oh! And mouse poo. I found mouse poo under the cupboard.

Then I realised how dark and scary it was in there and I began to worry. What if they never found me? And what if the mice came back at night to bite me? I was very brave. I didn't cry. I used my powers of mind control. I concentrated very hard and focused my brainwaves on Mr. D until I could sense that his were in sync with mine, then imagined him opening the door. And voila! He came to free me just in time, else I'd have starved. I think Linda is in VERY BIG trouble. It serves her right! He made her give me treats immediately to make up for the trauma I had suffered 'cos it was her fault I got locked in there.

24 August 2021

Aaaaaand we're back in lockdown again. Mr. D was NOT pleased when they announced it on the radio. He said he's had enough of this Covid bullship. It's best I don't repeat the things he said about the government 'cos I don't want them to come and arrest him.

Linda's also in a bad mood. She's still mad about the mess on the kitchen floor the day before yesterday and she's blaming me! It wasn't my fault AND I even tried to clean it up for her. How ungrateful!

25 August 2021

I lied. It was me who pushed the treat box off the shelf. I nudged the cupboard door open and got up in there. I knew I wasn't s'posed to, just like I knew we're not allowed in the garage. And I did a whole lot of other naughties too, too many to mention (but not as many as Judi). I'm too embarrassed to talk about it. Let's just say there was poo involved, and not by accident. On purpose.

I had every intention of turning over a new leaf and becoming a good kitty this week. I really did, I promise. I just don't think I can do it on my own. I need help because naughty is so much fun, and it's tempting to give in to every naughty urge. Let's face it, it's way, way easier to naughty than it is to good. But then I always feel so terrible after I've naughtied, and it's not worth it in the end.

26 August 2021

I had a long chat with my sister, Candy, 'cos she's always good and sweet and nice. She gave me some very sound advice. She says the only perfect being is G.O.D. and I shouldn't feel sad 'cos I failed. I've already done the hard part. I've admitted my failure and that I can't do it on my own. Now I should ask G.O.D. to help me 'cos He's very forgiving when we admit our mistakes, and everyone makes mistakes. It's not the end of the world.

I don't know G.O.D. very well ('cept that He sent me here on this mission to Earth), but Candy says G.O.D. would like nothing better than for me to get to know Him as my true friend 'cos He loves me very much and He already knows everything that's in my heart and mind, every moment of every day. Wow! What an amazing superpower!

I think this is what hoomins call religion, but Candy says it isn't at all. 'Cos religion is man-made and something completely different. It's all about rules and restrictions and it makes us feel guilty 'cos it's impossible to obey all the rules all the time. Religion makes us hate each other and fight with one another 'cos there are so many religions, and they don't all have the same rules. Candy says religion and politics are very similar 'cos they're both all about power and control.

But being close to G.O.D. is something entirely different 'cos it's about mutual love, not rules. And when you truly love someone, all you want is to please them. So, I'm going to ask G.O.D. to reveal Himself to my heart. I want to be close to Him all the time so I can bring Him joy.

I think it's prudent to be honest with myself about my failures though. I'll start a list. I'm good at lists.

Naughty or Nice?

- ✓ Kindness.
- ✓ Patience.
- ✓ Humility.
- ✓ Gentleness.
- ☐ _____
- ✗ Telling lies.
- ✗ Selfishness.
- ✗ Boastfulness.
- ✗ Cheating.
- ☐ _____

27 August 2021

After I spoke to G.O.D. last night I fell into a deep, peaceful sleep and I had an amazing dream about a beautiful white cat with golden wings. I think she was an angel cat. It wasn't Judi 'cos she's no angel, that's for sure!

28 August 2021

There was a little mishap with the plant again. But this time I made sure Linda knew it was me. I didn't blame Callie.

Linda said, "Awww don't be sad, Gina. Accidents happen, Sweetie." I felt so relieved!

My sister is my friend !!!

29 August 2021

I love my big sister. I'm so lucky to have a sister like her. I love all my sisters, but Callie is our big sister, and she looks out for all of us. She may be a little cranky and sometimes she's quite rude, but her heart's in the right place.

George did well to arrange this mission for me. He knew Callie and I would get along well. Me an' Callie and Linda are almost done writing George's book[3]. It's a beautiful love story. Callie still misses George very much, but I think it's been cathartic for her to tell his story and I'm glad I could help. He's such a handsome cat. I think the cover of his book looks pretty good.

George will never be forgotten. Sometimes I just lie snuggled up close to Callie and let her talk. We have these long conversations about George. I think it gives her much comfort that I'm here to listen.

[3] *The Book of George (An Angel Cats Series book), Write Impression, 2021*

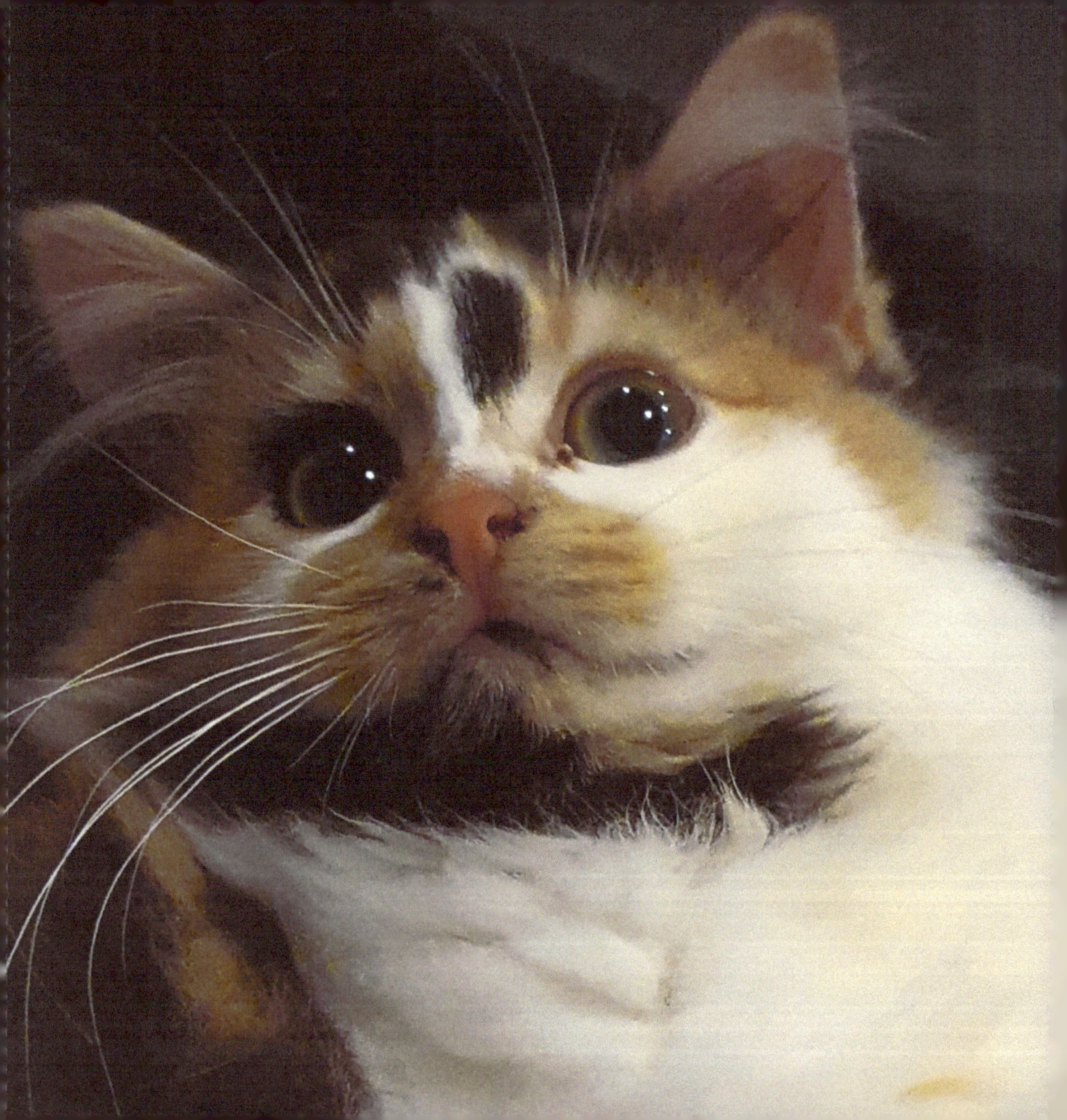

30 August 2021

Breakfast was late AGAIN today. Callie woke Linda up by standing on her chest and complaining about the service in this place. It is pretty poor, I must admit. Linda said something that sounded like: "Ouch! Gerroff-me-dammit-it's-still-dark-lemme-zleeeeep!" but Callie wouldn't budge and then Mr. D got up to make the coffee and Callie followed him to the kitchen and put in a formal complaint about the service, so he gave us all treats and said we mustn't tell Linda 'cos she will be very cross if she finds out why Callie's diet isn't working.

Then Callie asked if Linda was hibernating. I had no idea what that long word means, so, I had a look in the dictionary:

Hibernate: an extended period of remaining inactive or indoors.

Well, that's exactly what Linda is doing! She spends all day on the computer, tapping away at the keys. If that's not being lazy and inactive indoors, then I dunno what is.

Linda says she's not being lazy: she's doing the finishing touches on George's book. That's just ridiculous! Callie and I told her the story of George AGES and ages ago, and I could have told her another three stories if she wasn't so slow at making books out of them. Why does it take her so long to catch up? Sometimes I think I should just do it all myself. Geez. How hard can it be?

Oops... when I think thoughts like this, then G.O.D. doesn't feel very near.

31 August 2021

Uh oh! I messed up again. I felt pretty bad after my rant about Linda yesterday. I shouldn't have been so hard on her. I mustn't complain about the service 'cos she does try. I showed her I was sorry for being so demanding by letting her tickle my tummy. I know she likes doing that, and it is quite nice for me too. Now I feel better again. I guess G.O.D. speaks to me through my conscience, telling me when I'm making Him sad.

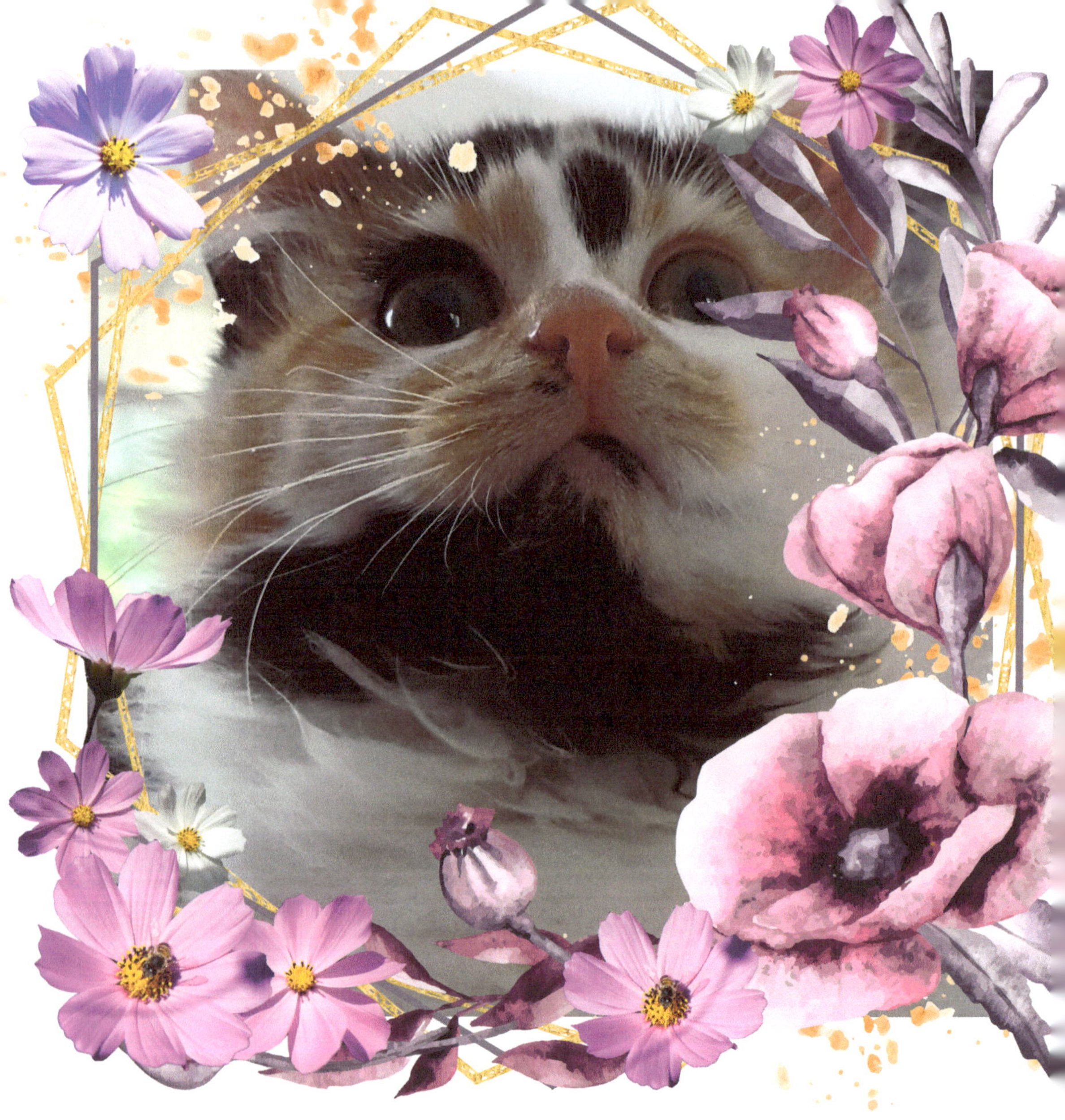

1 September 2021

It's Spring Day! YAY!!! The days will be getting warmer and longer.

I hope I get to play outside in the sunshine, but Callie says not to hold my breath.

I dunno what she means. Why would I want to hold my breath when I'm outside in the fresh air? Surely breathing in fresh, healthy air is the whole point of being outside?

2 September 2021

Apparently, I'm not allowed outside. Ever. Linda says it's too dangerous, and after George, she'll never let another cat enjoy the outdoors unsupervised again. Personally, I think she's being over-protective because I know how to take care of myself.

Oh! And I'm getting a spade on the 10th. What's the point of giving me a spade if I can't go outside to use it? I don't understand. I asked Callie about this spade business, and she just laughed. What's so funny?

3 September 2021

Linda keeps talking about this spade I'm getting. I'm not sure if she intends for me to come and work in the garden with her, or what? I thought I wasn't allowed outside.

And I don't know why she keeps banging on about me getting a spade before going on heat. Huh?!

I LIKE lying in front of the Magic Blowy Box[4] and getting heated by the nice, warm air. What's so bad about that?

4 September 2021

I was called pretty today... well, actually, the full statement was: "You're pretty annoying, Gina! Get off the table." But, hey... I only focus on the positive.

---

[4] See The Journal of Agent Gina Ginger Knickers (Phase One: Advent and Subjugation), p.5, A Guide to Gina-Speak, Part 1

5 September 2021

Interpretive sleeping is like interpretive dance, and the best place to do it is on a hoomin lap. This is not to be confused with lap dancing, though.

6 September 2021

Another vitally important use of the hoomin lap is, of course, as a bathing platform.

Used in this way (if you can get your hoomin to keep still), you can have a very comfortable and relaxing bath.

7 September 2021

I wonder if real mice taste like catnip mice? 'Cos if they do, I am SO going to catch me a real mouse someday. When I sniff and chew my catnip mousey, Linda says I go a bit loopy. I have no idea what she's talking about, but I must say, catnip mousies make me feel very chilled and happy.

8 September 2021

Me and Callie help each other with our daily grooming routines. She washes me, and I wash her. I don't mind washing her face and ears, but I'm not that keen on washing her butt. She said George used to do that for her, and she'd return the favour, but I think that's taking it too far. She and George must have been very, very intimate... um... er... "friends". Very!

9 September 2021

Linda does this really weird thing. Mr. D does it too, and I'm wondering if all hoomins do, or is it just these two? They seem to LOVE wiping their hands on me... and on Callie, Candy, Judi and, apparently, all the others! I don't mean just one wipe and they're done. Nope. They do it repeatedly: wipe... wipe... wipe... wipe... Look, I'm not really complaining. I quite like it. I'm just wondering why they do this compulsive hand-wiping thing on our backs, sometimes for hours and hours?

Like when I'm warming Linda's lap for her in the evenings while they gaze at the Magic Window[5]. Of course, I can't help myself, and my purr motor switches itself on automatically. But this just encourages her, and she goes at it even more enthusiastically.

However, it is more than a little annoying when I'm in deep sleep and Linda sneaks up on me. She plants a kiss on my nose then starts wiping her hands on me. This makes me feel a little resentful 'cos it cuts into my sleep time, but I guess she's helping me learn about patience. Sigh...

I wish she'd be more considerate when I've just had a good wash and I'm all nice and clean and fresh. Does she really have to wipe her dirty hands on me, 'cos then I have to start all over again? It takes so much effort to maintain all this glorious floof. I spend hours and hours having to wash stinky hand smells off of it. Do you have any idea how gross things like hand lotion taste? I don't think she realises I can taste everything she touches and sometimes it's not pleasant.

I don't mind if she wipes her hands on me after she's been cooking, but it's really yucky after she's done the washing or dishes. Or when Mr. D's been tinkering about with stuff in the garage.

[5] *See The Journal of Agent Gina Ginger Knickers (Phase One: Advent and Subjugation), p.20, A Guide to Gina-Speak, Part 2*

10 September 2021

I'd like to register a formal complaint with Planet Cat.

1) I wasn't allowed to have breakfast this morning.

2) I was misled by Linda into thinking a spade was something entirely different.

3) I'm not at all sure I approve of the dragons and unicorns rampaging through our house at the moment. They're everywhere!

I am so, so, SO sleepy! And groggy. Zzzzzz.... Zzzzzz... Zzz

11 September 2021

Callie let me have the prime spot-on Linda's lap last night, and afterwards me an' my big sister sent all the purple dragons packing. I wouldn't have minded if the pink unicorns stayed, but they left too. I'm full of energy today. Among other things, I've already shredded a pack of paper serviettes Linda inadvertently left on the table, and I've knocked two of her kitty ornaments off the dresser. It's okay, she does have super glue and she's quite resourceful. I'm bouncing off the walls and I eated almost a whole tub of Jimbo's since my return from the vet. BTW, I'm very disappointed that nobody 'splained to me what a spade really is but, I'm spayed now and officially a big girl.

Today I absolutely HAVE to keep Linda anchored to her desk and laptop, working on George's tribute book[6] which also includes lots of other Rainbow Bridge kitties. She MUST finish it this weekend. Lots of people are waiting for it.

[6]*The Book of George (An Angel Cats Series book), Write Impression, 2021*

12 September 2021

Oh, my word! There's such a pretty kitty out there in the garden. I hope she'll come inside and play with me.

No, wait! IT'S ME!!! I'm such a silly billy. It's my reflection in the window. Tee Hee...

13 September 2021

Aaaaand, just like that, it's done! George's book is finished and so is this notebook. I'll have to continue my journal in a new book. In the meantime, you can get in touch if you'd like to order any of my books, including all the ones I did to benefit various kitty charities.

Email us if you'd like any of these, (or if you'd like to chat about anything), and I'll get Linda to reply. You can also connect with me on Facebook.

cats@deanes.co.nz

facebook.com/TheNotSoCrazyCatLady

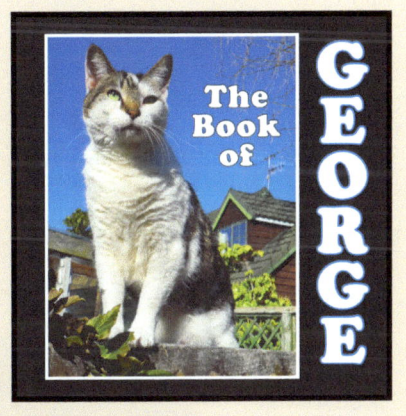

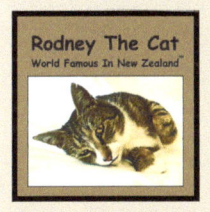

Milton Keynes UK
Ingram Content Group UK Ltd.
UKHW050617260424
441793UK00002B/9